baby name

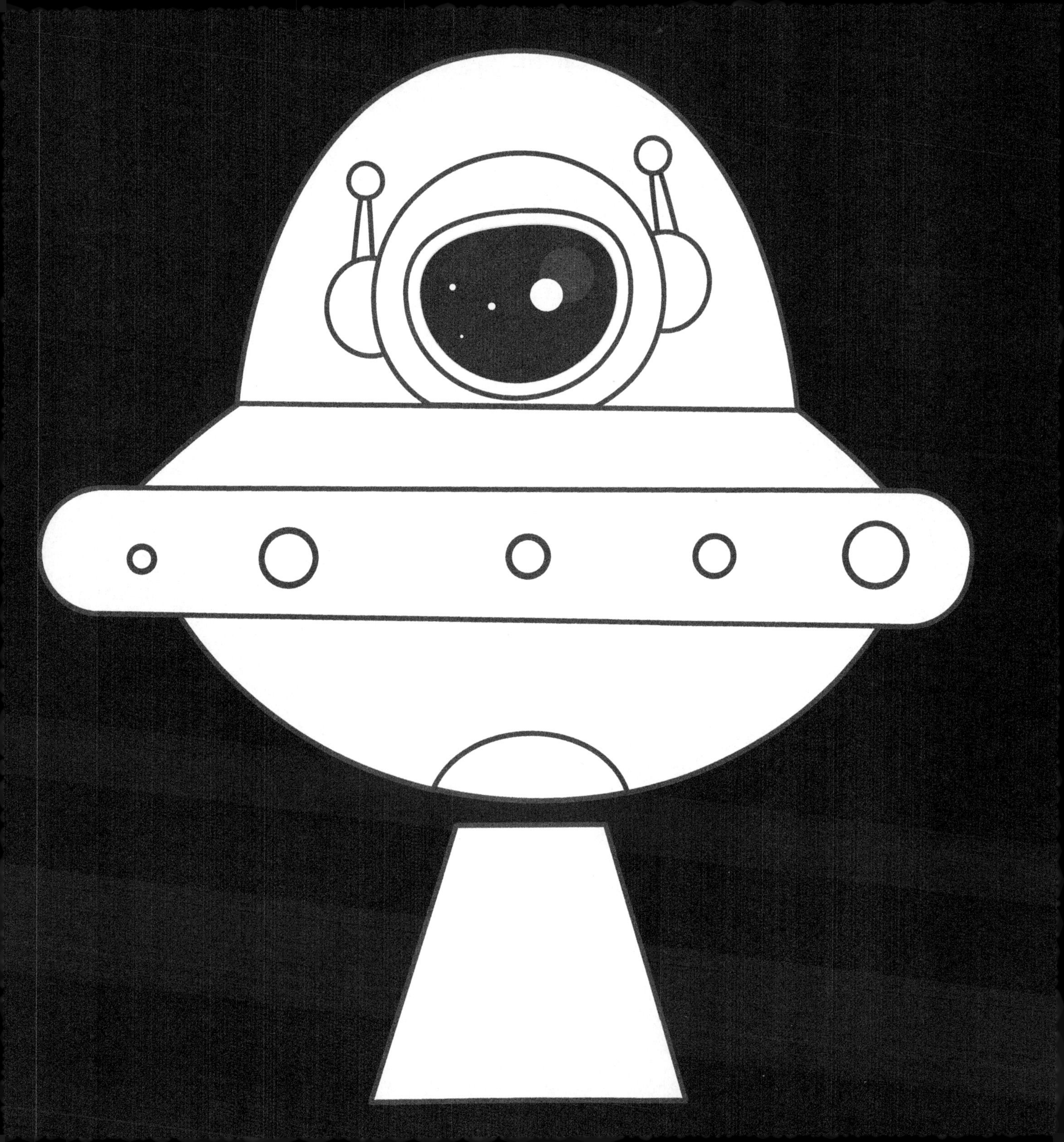

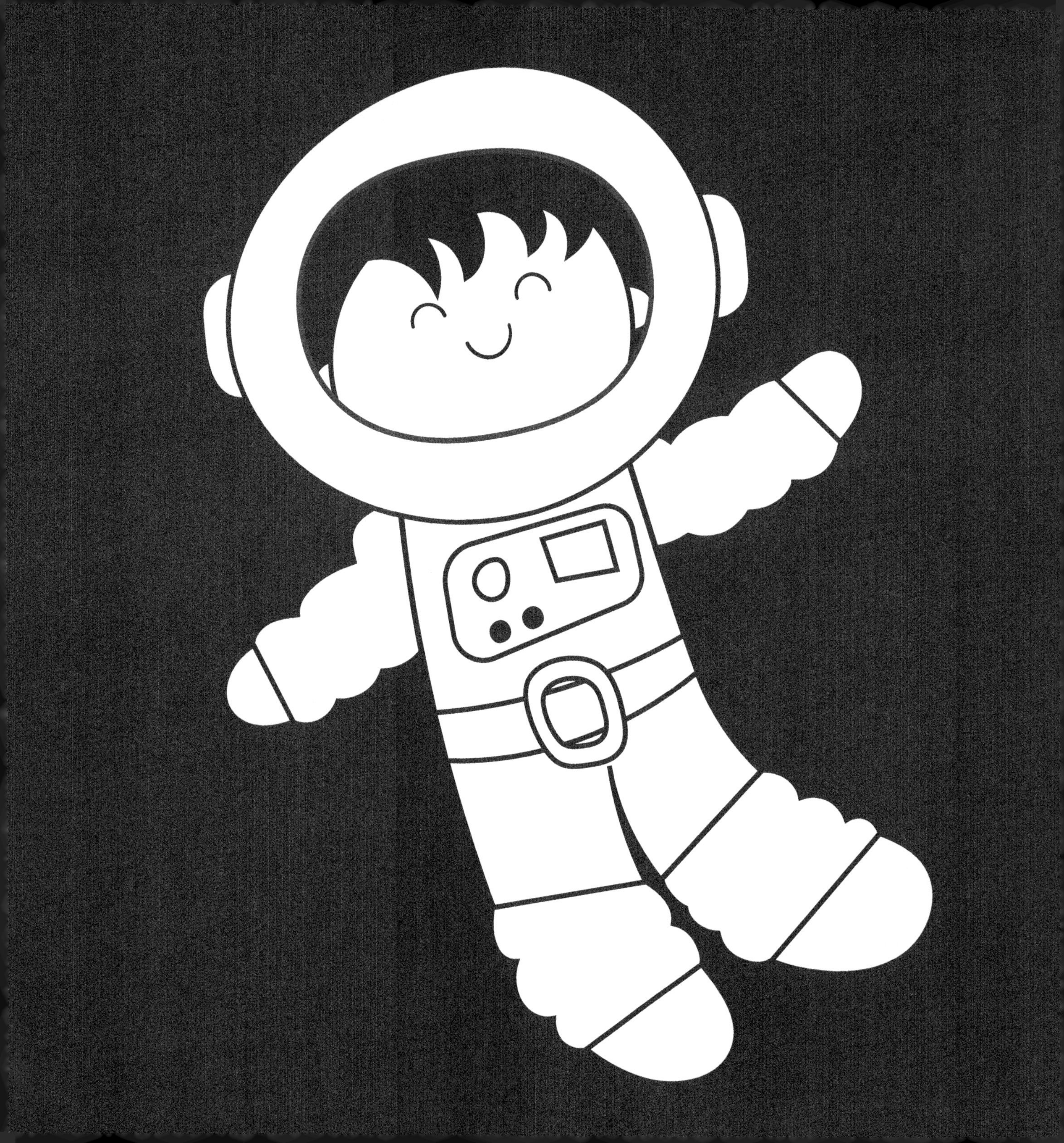

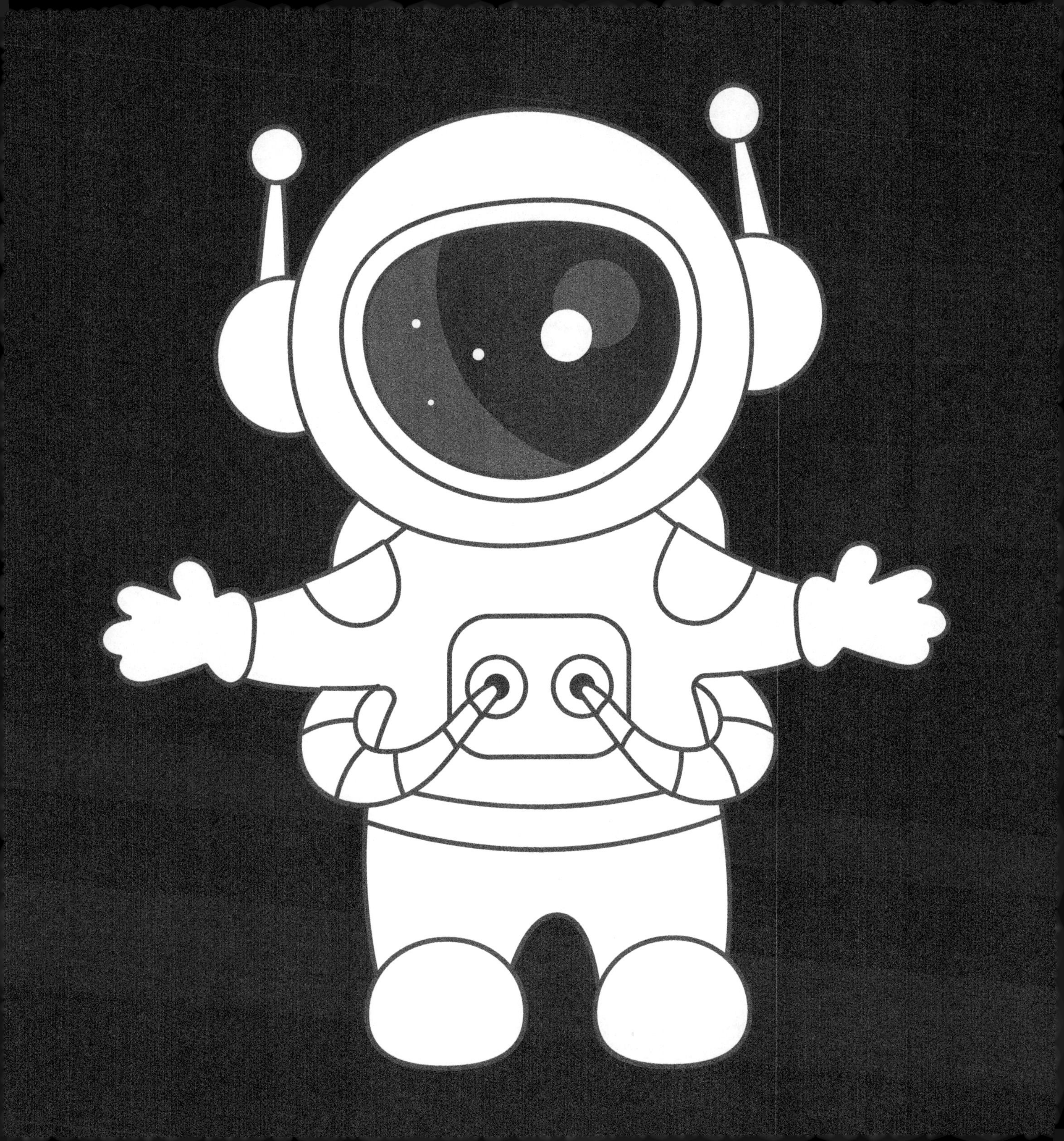

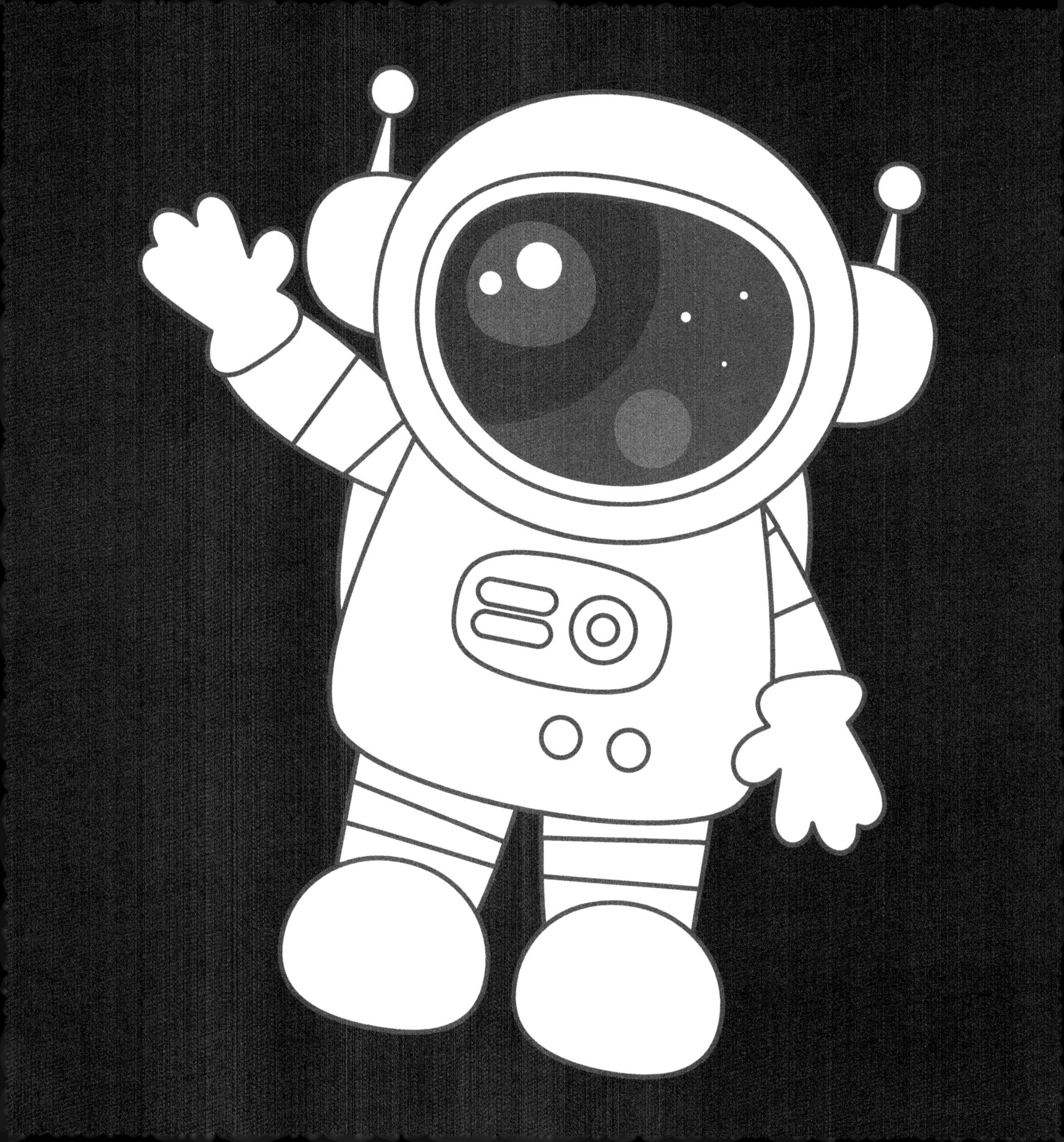

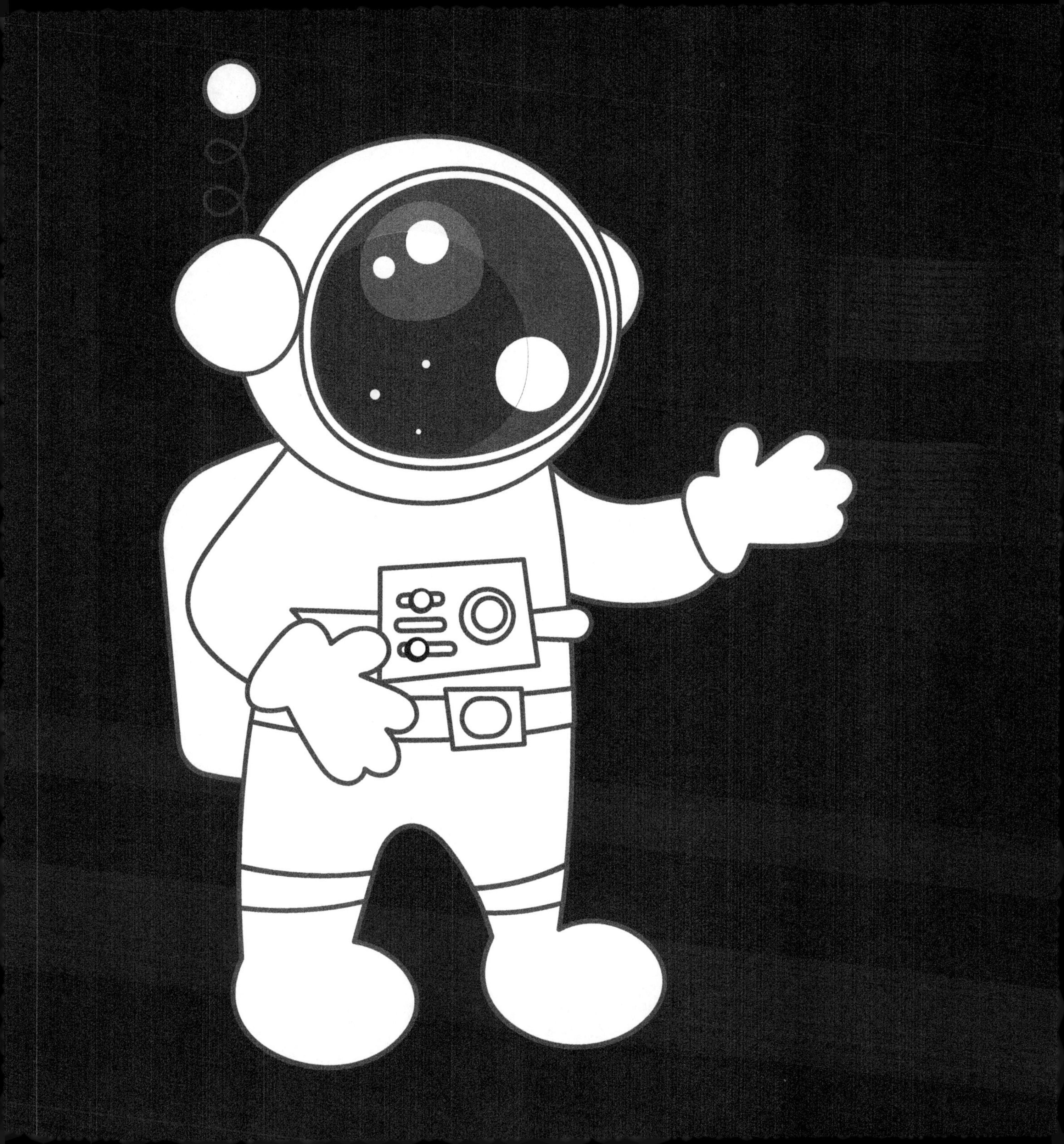

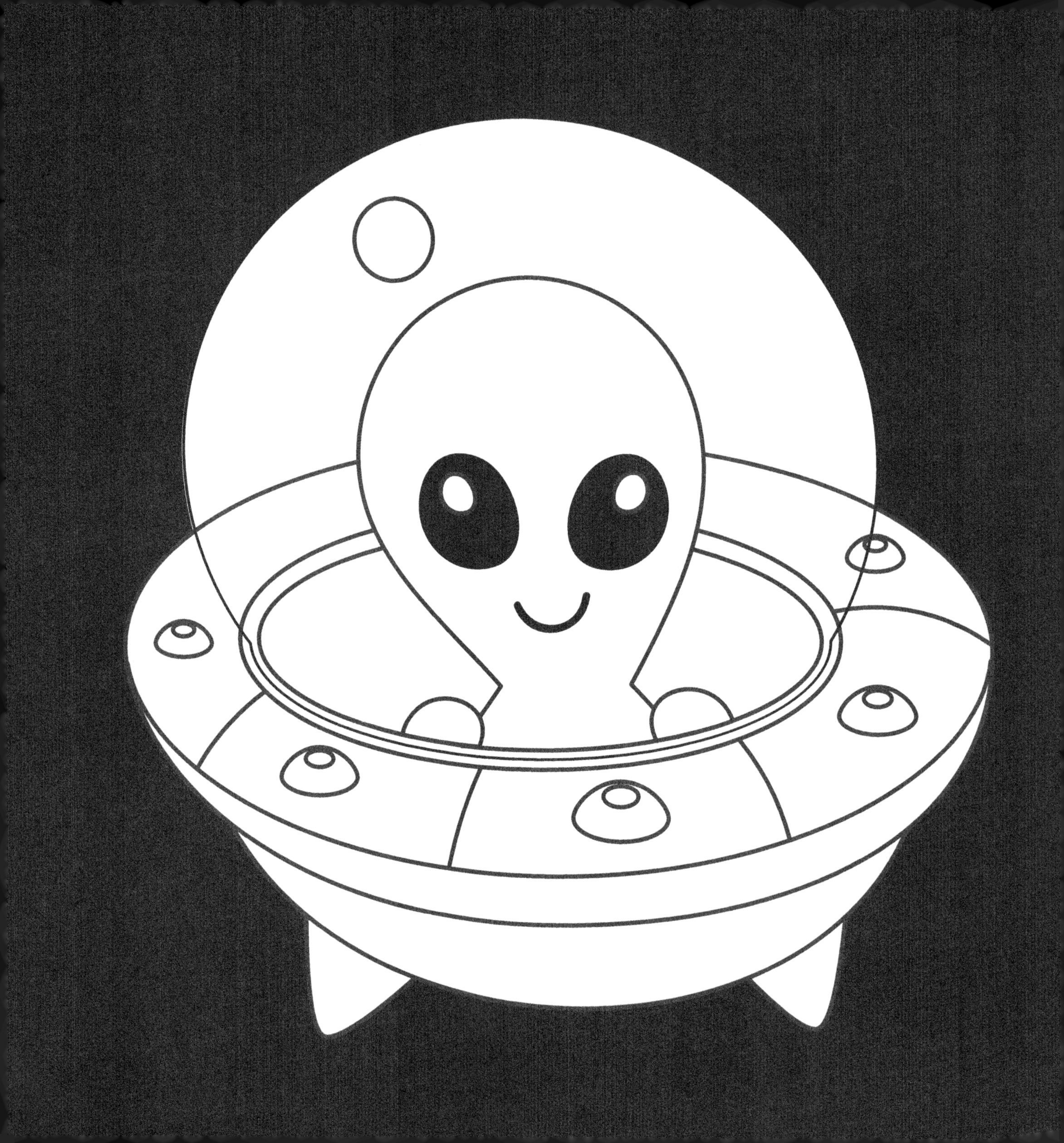

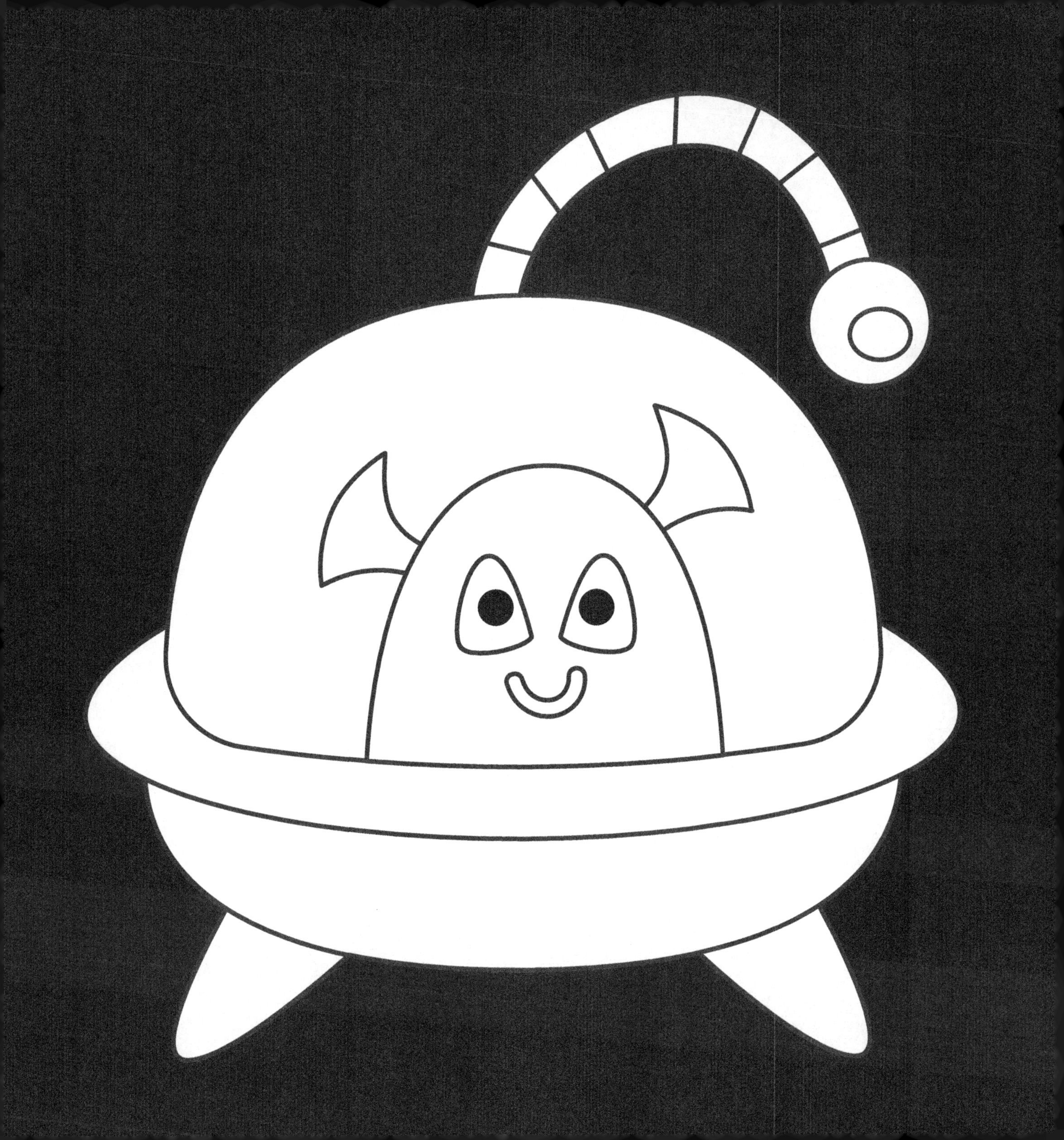

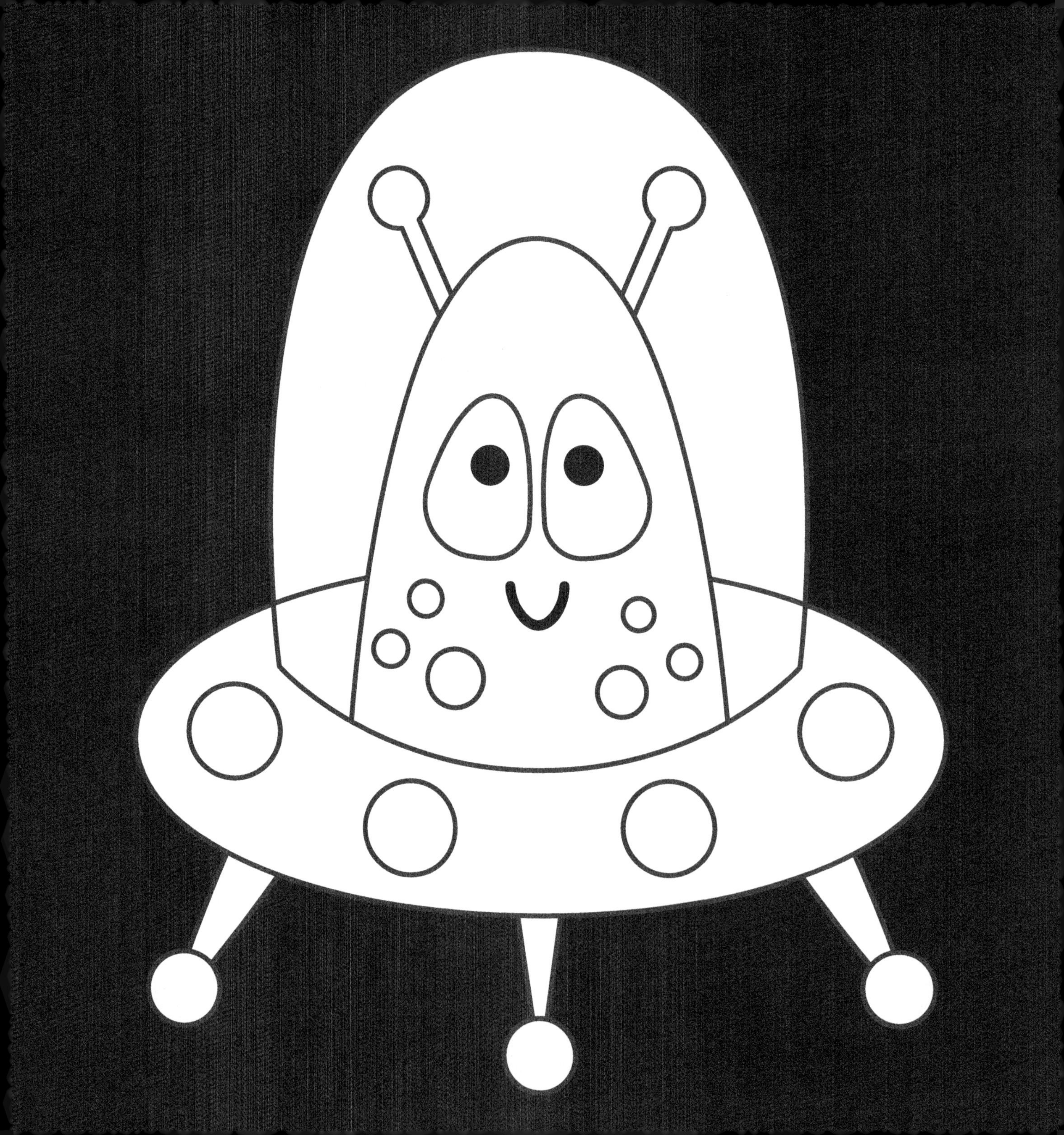

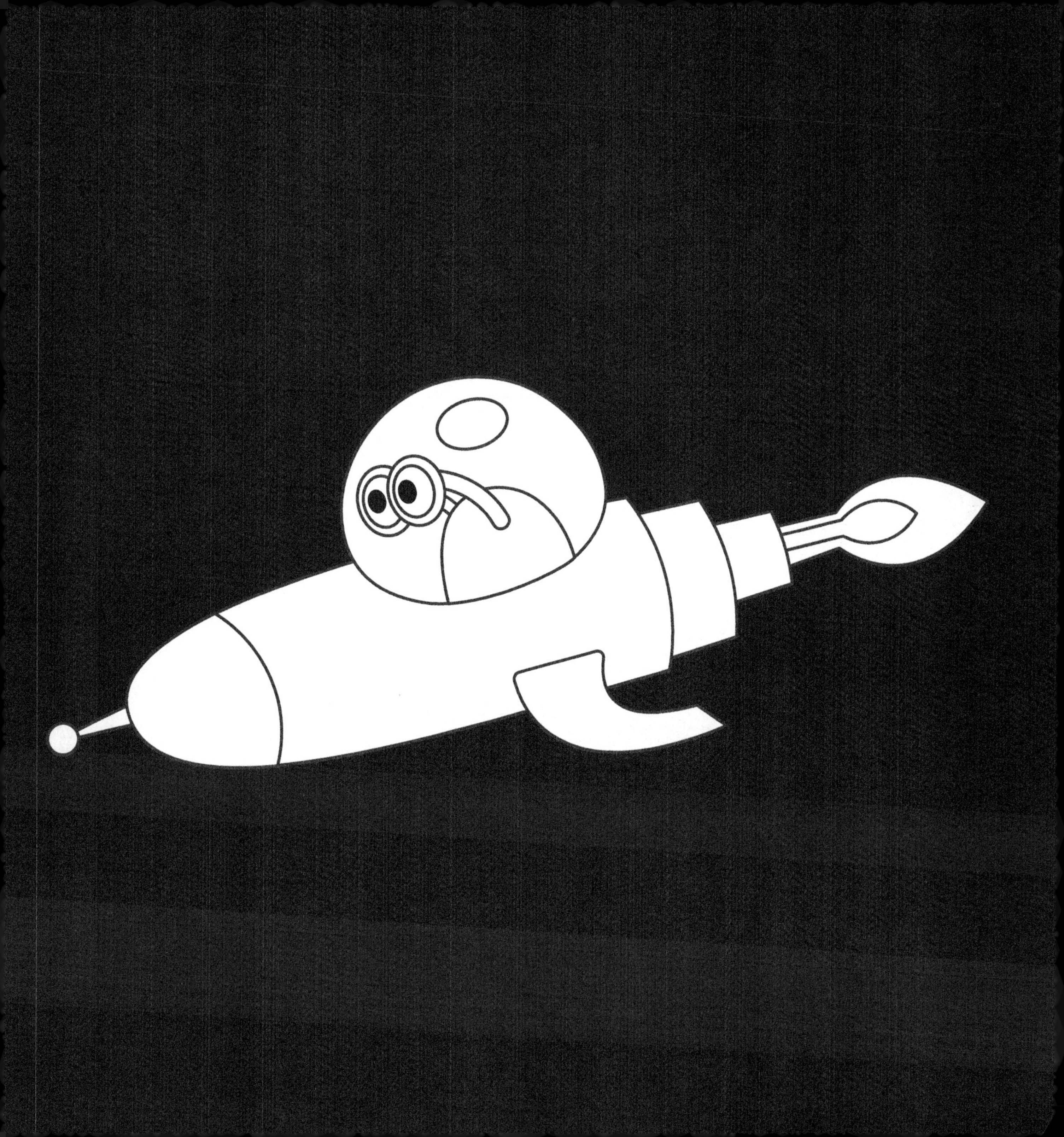

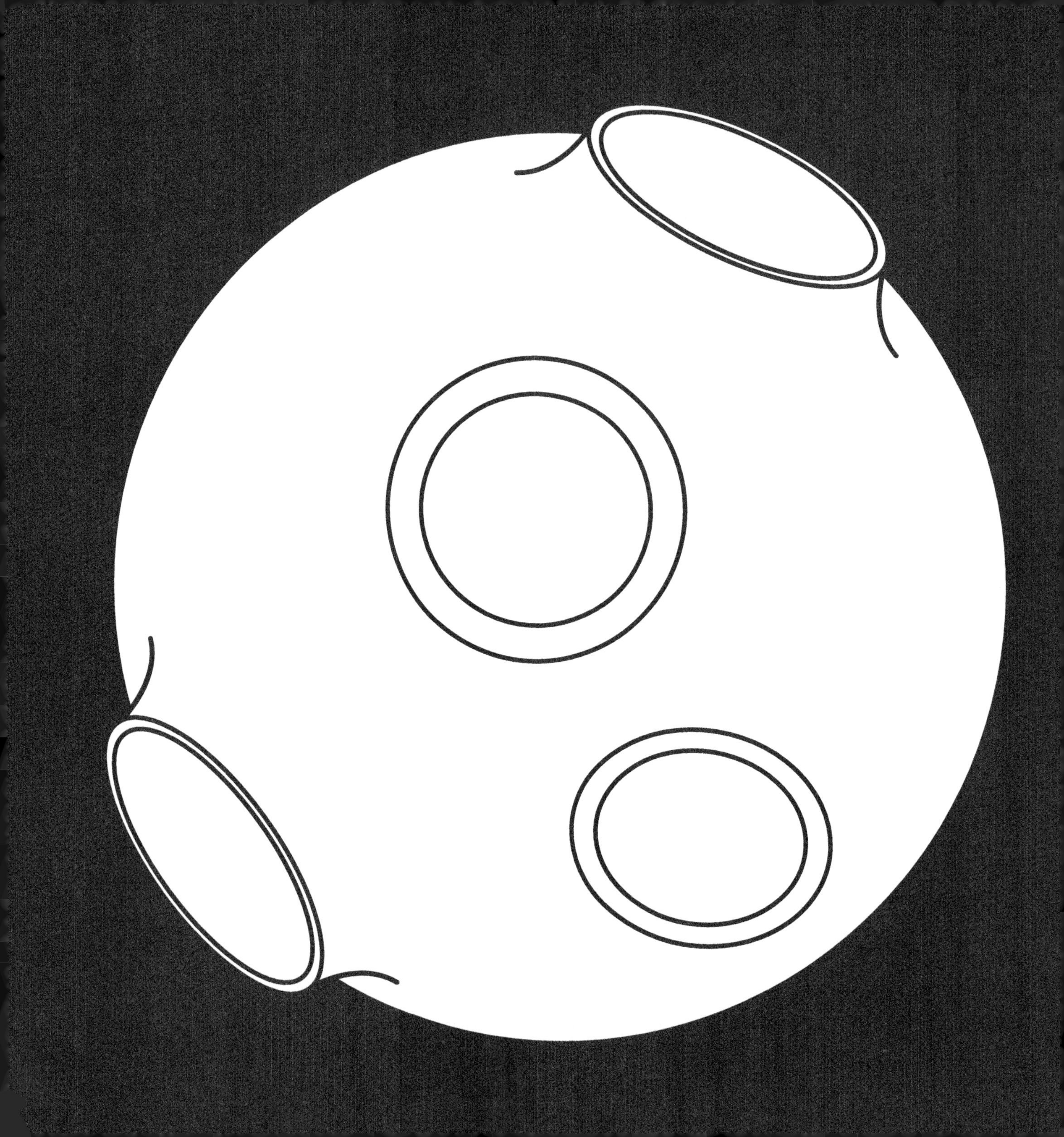

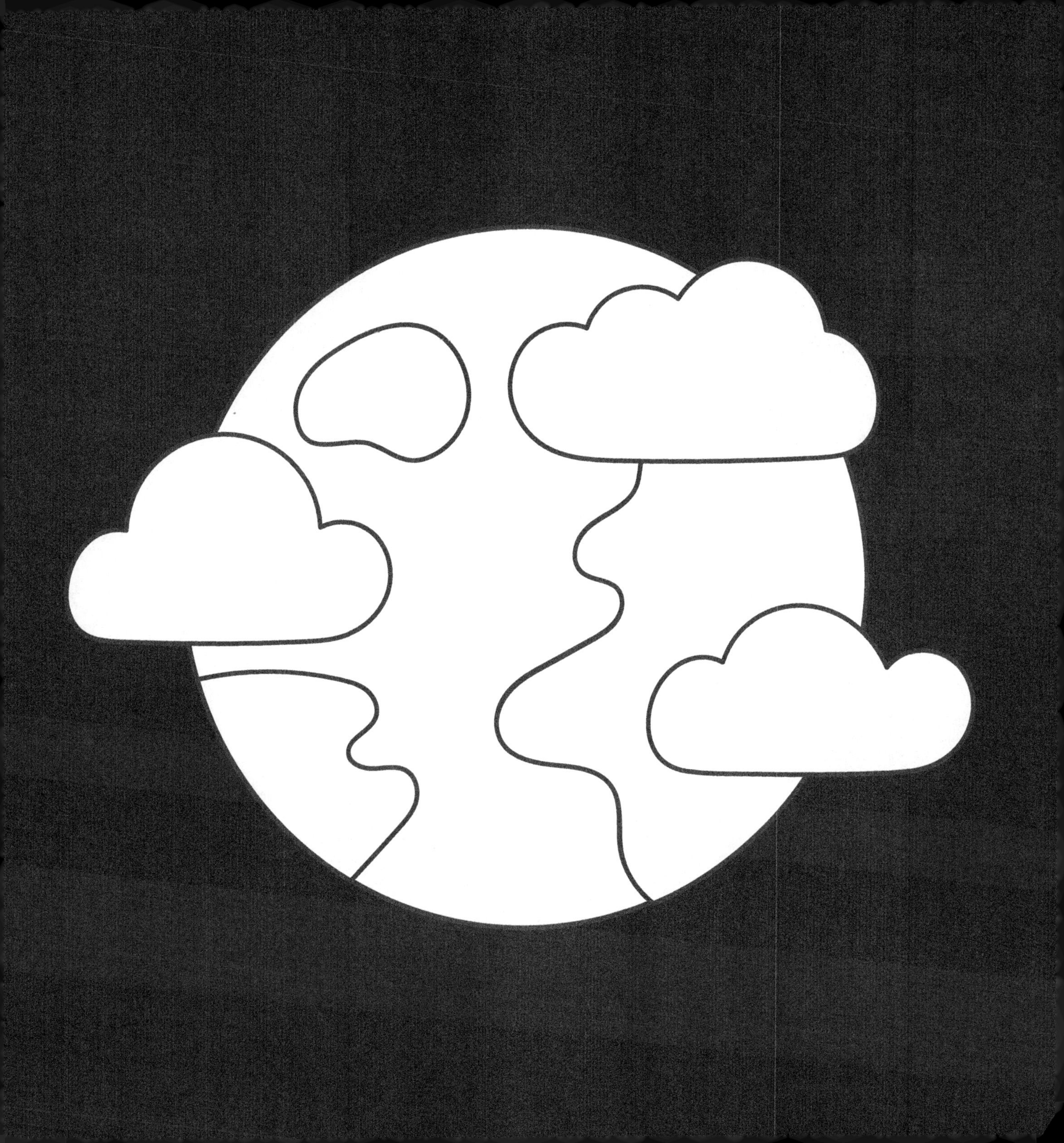

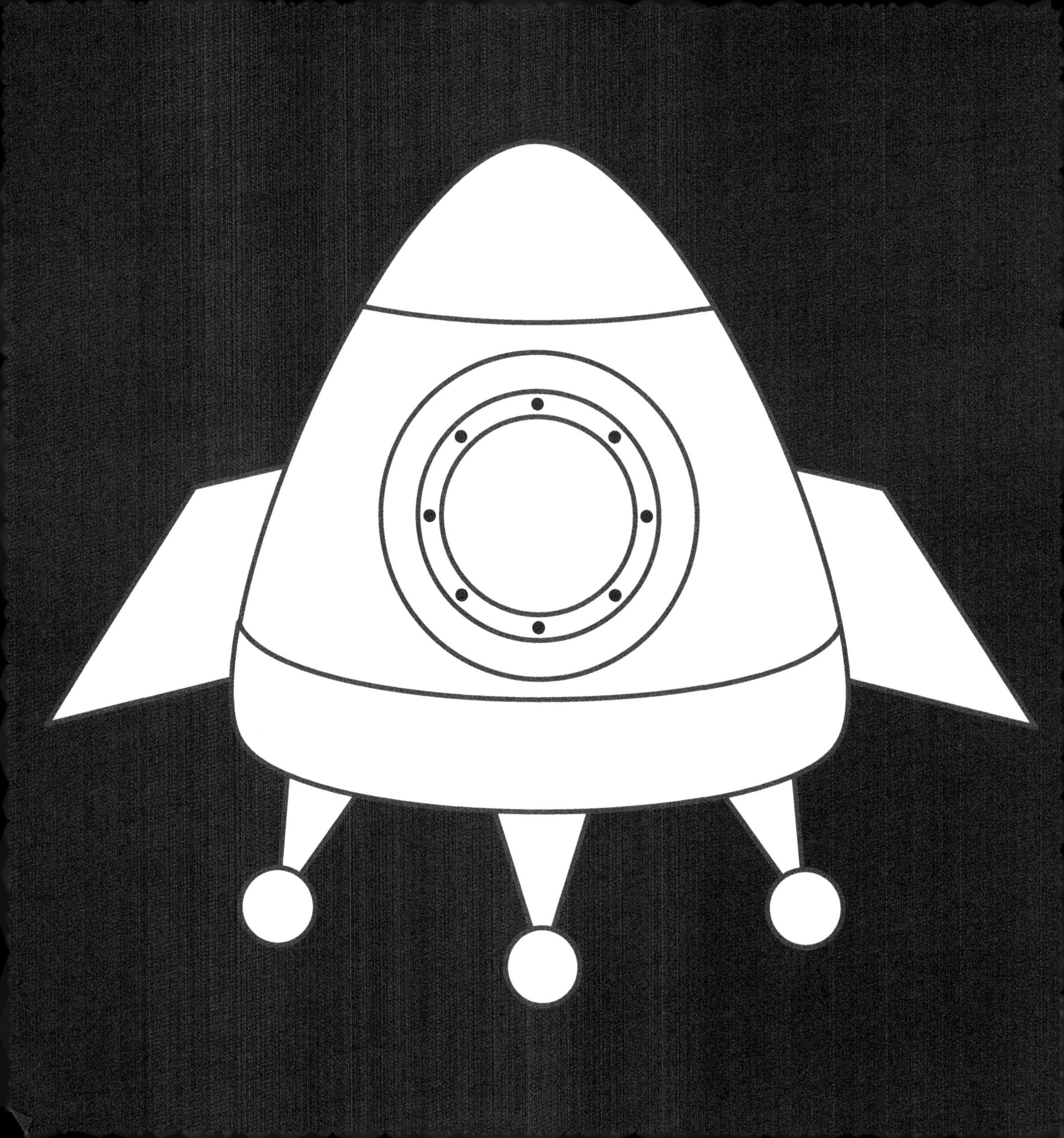

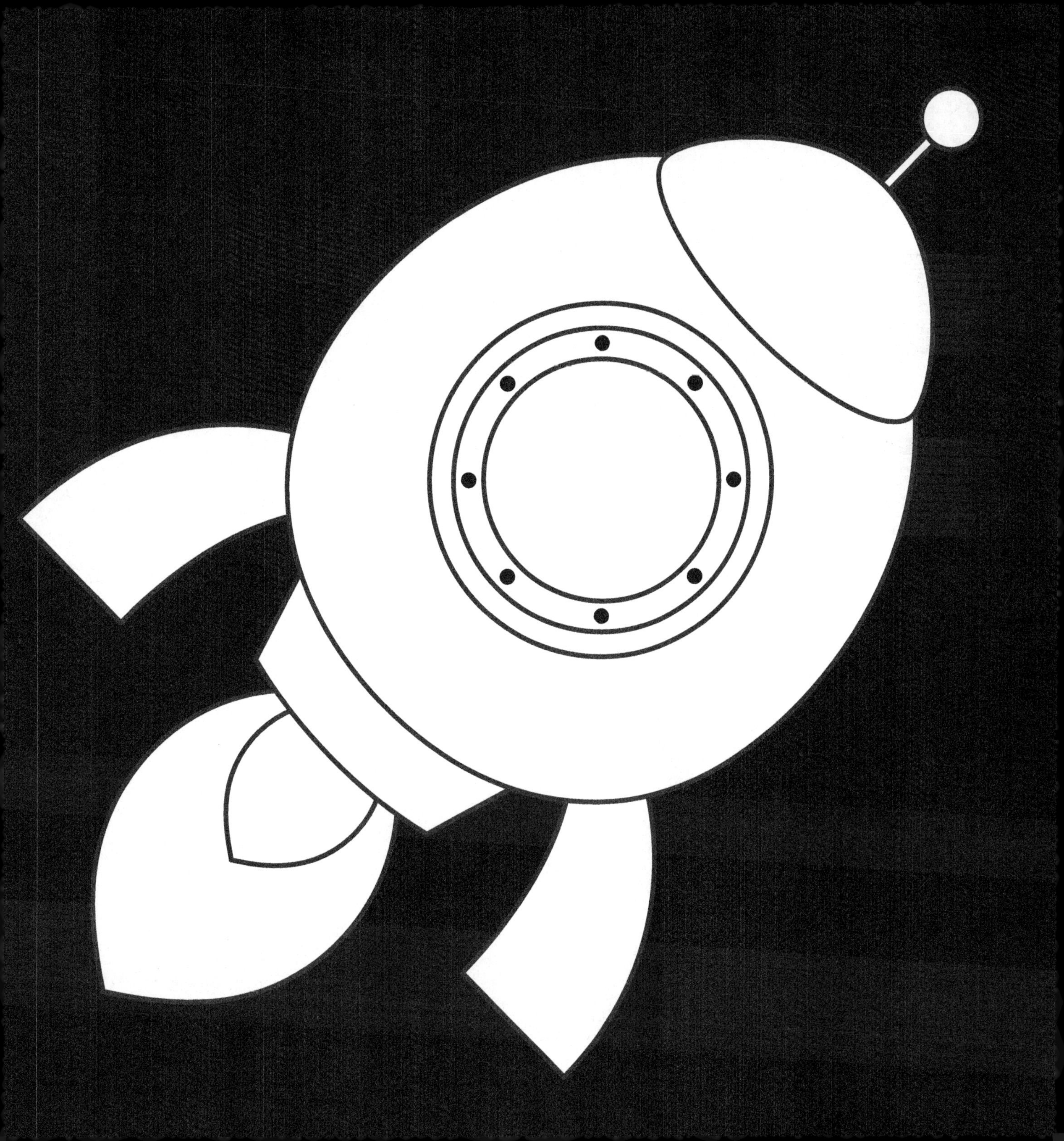

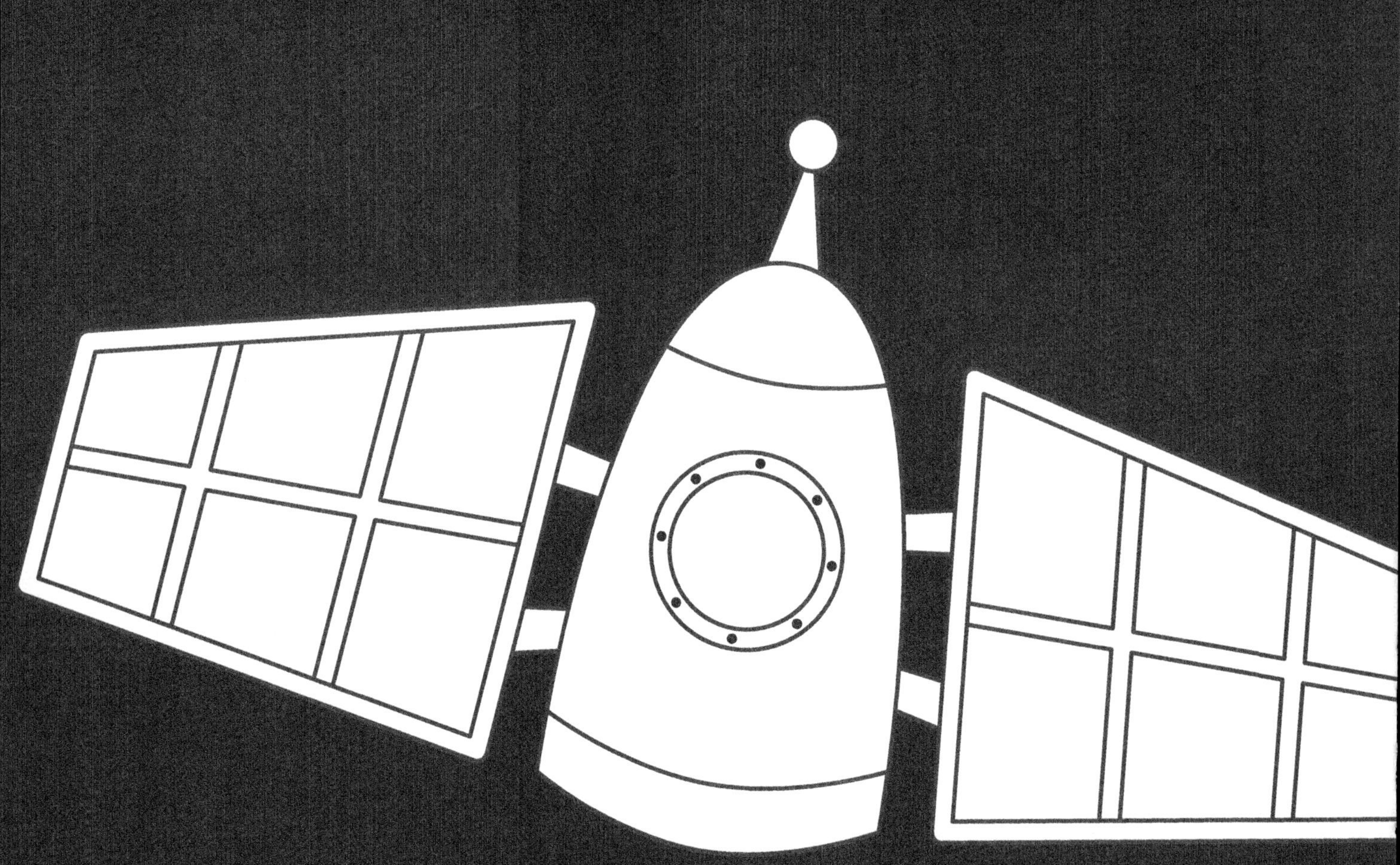

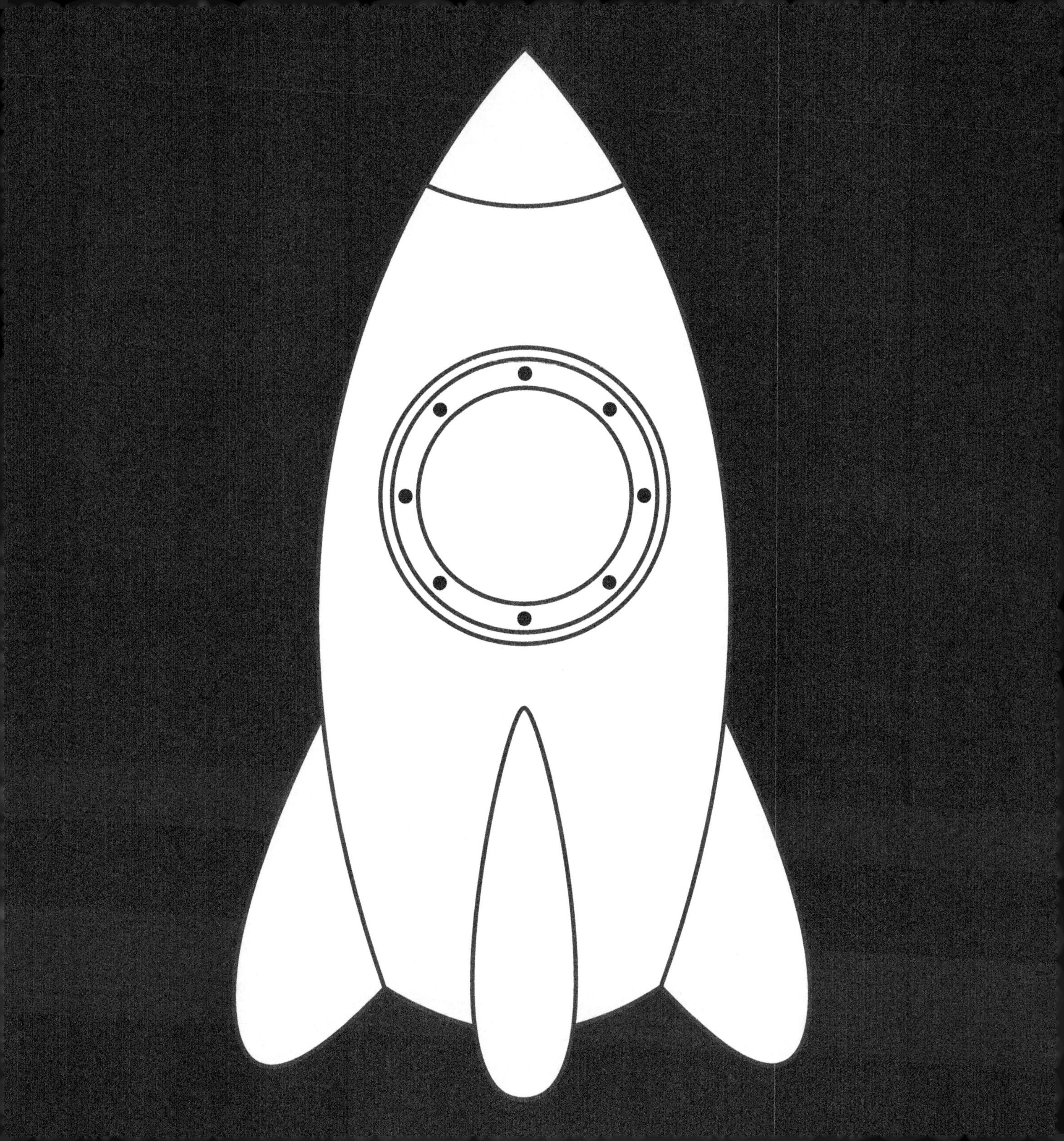

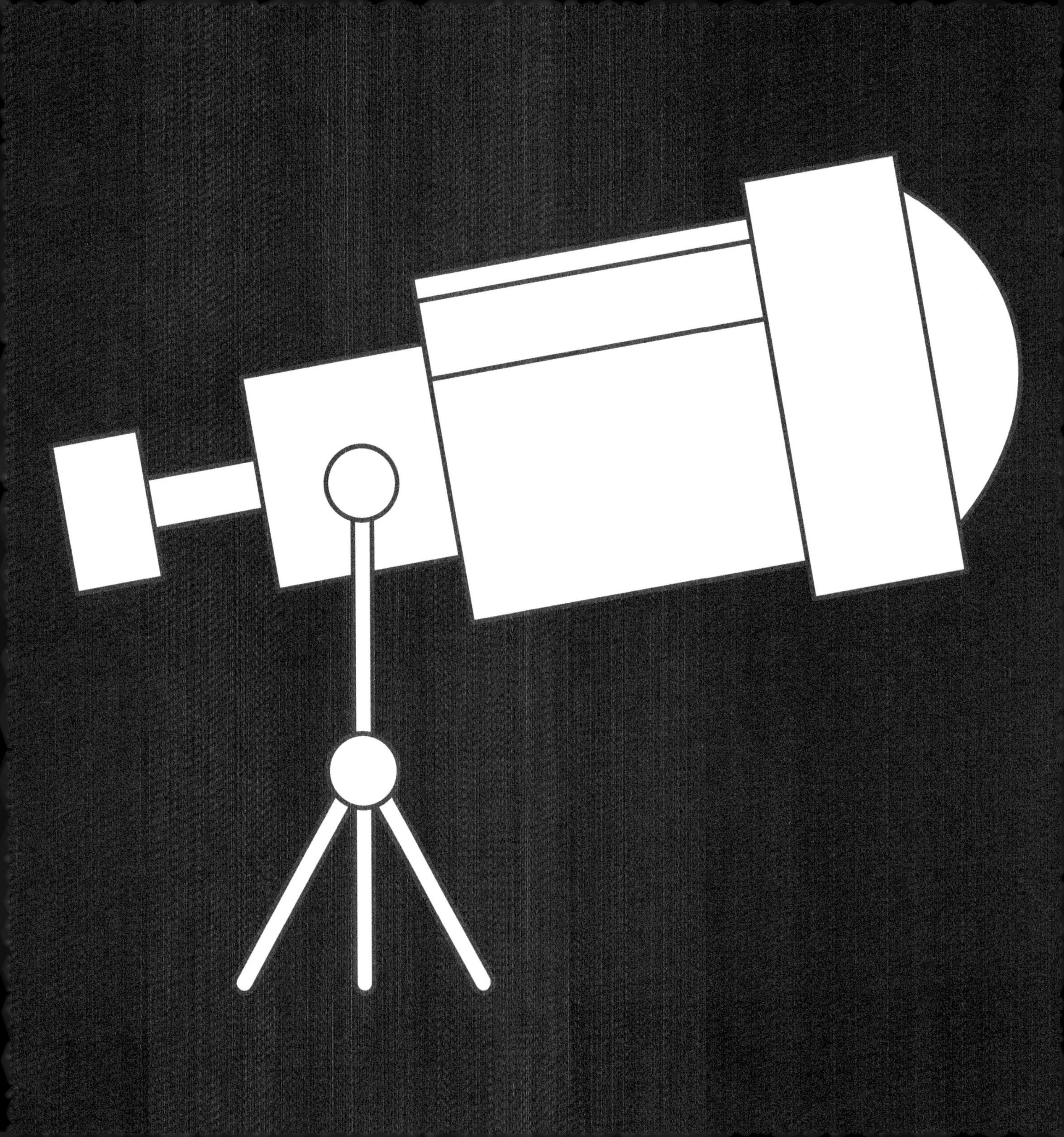

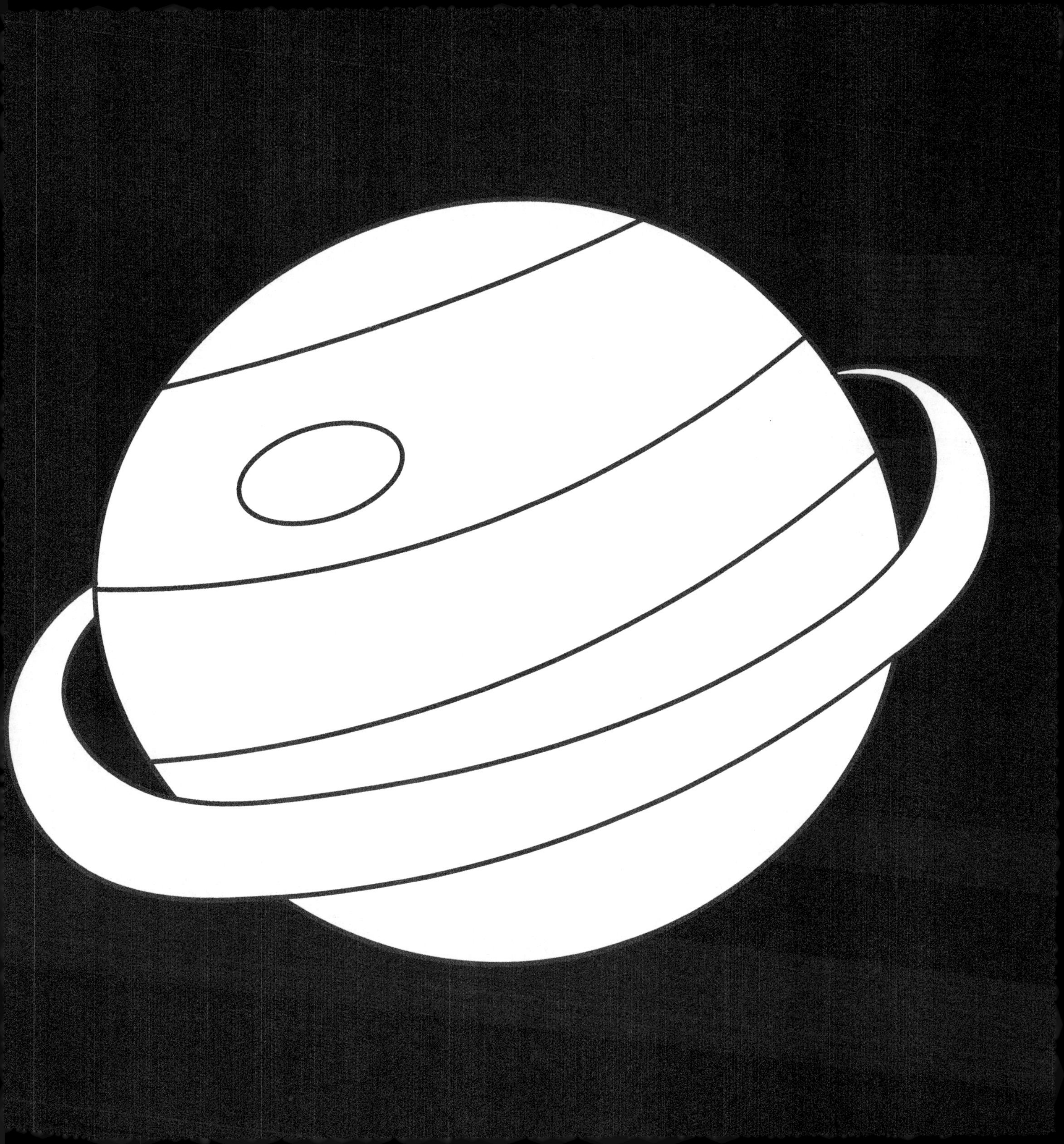

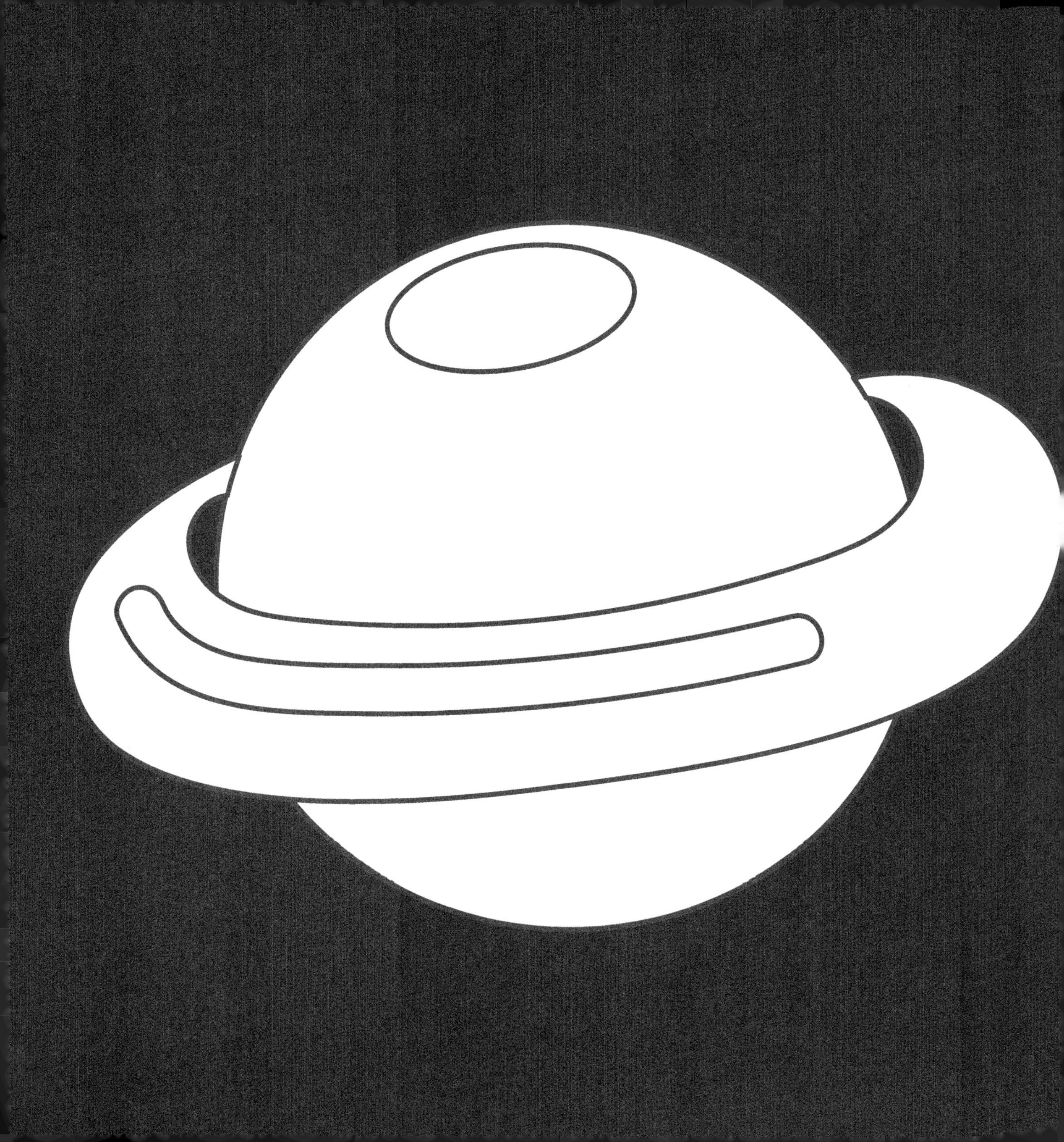

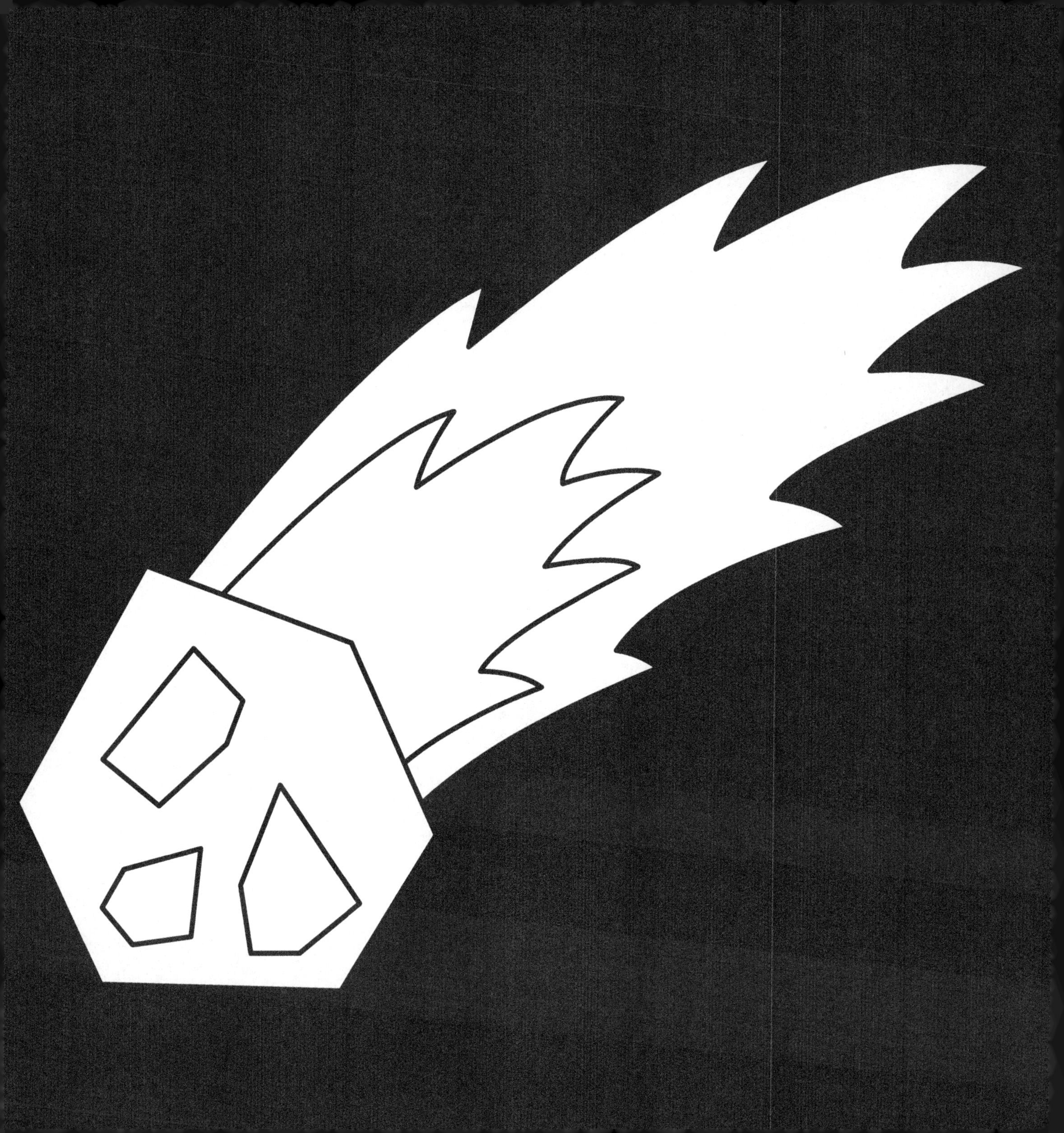

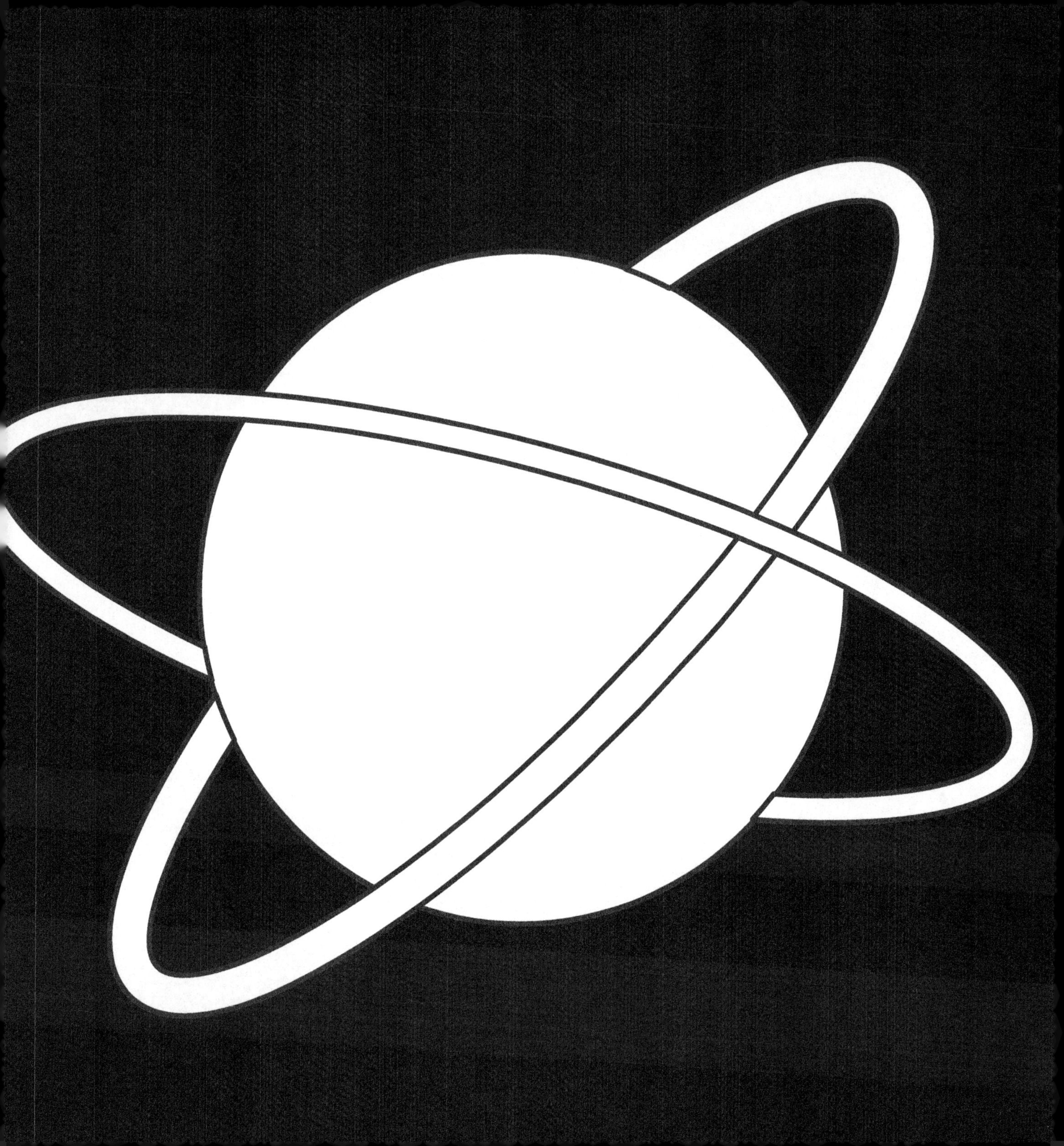

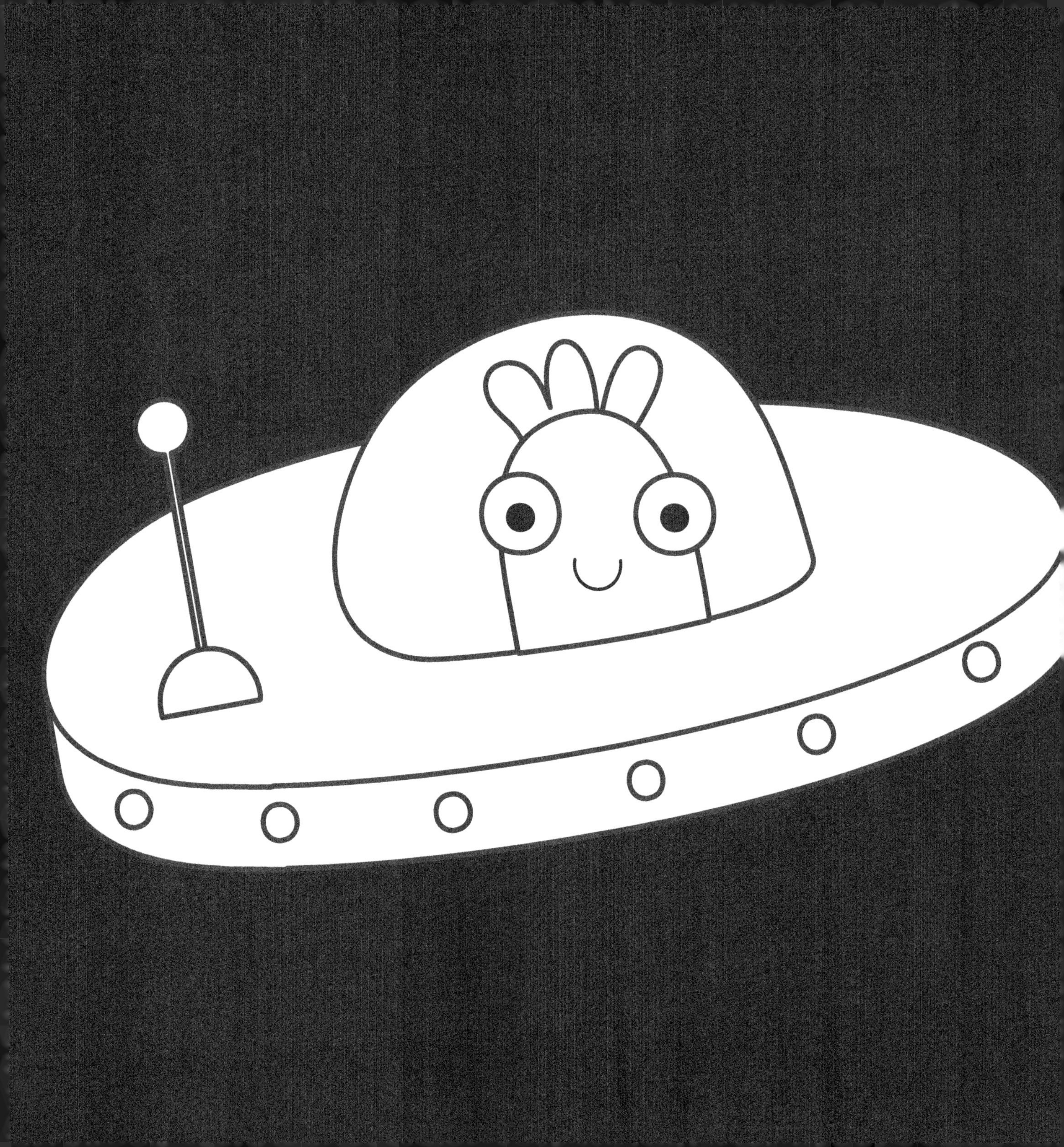

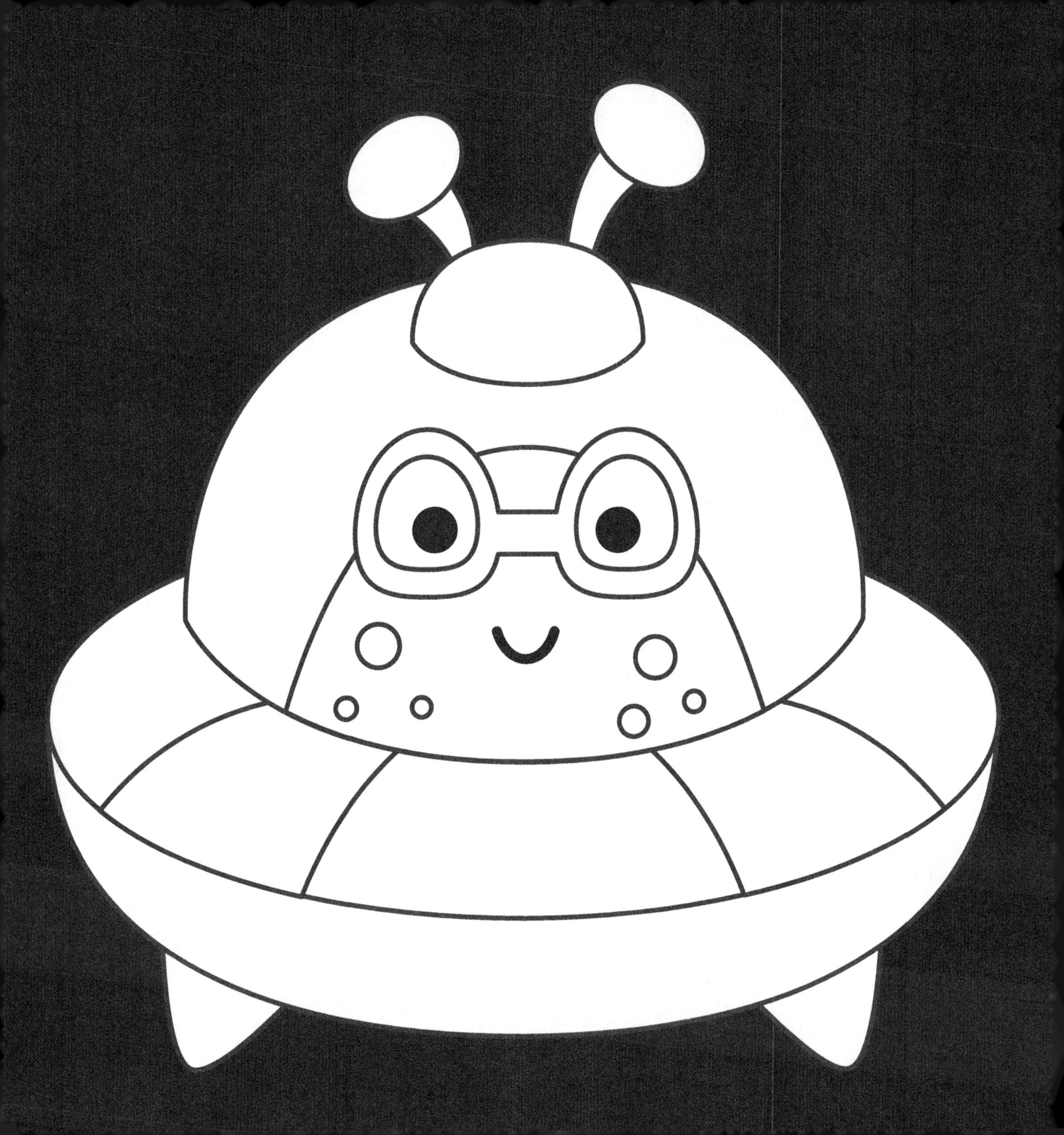

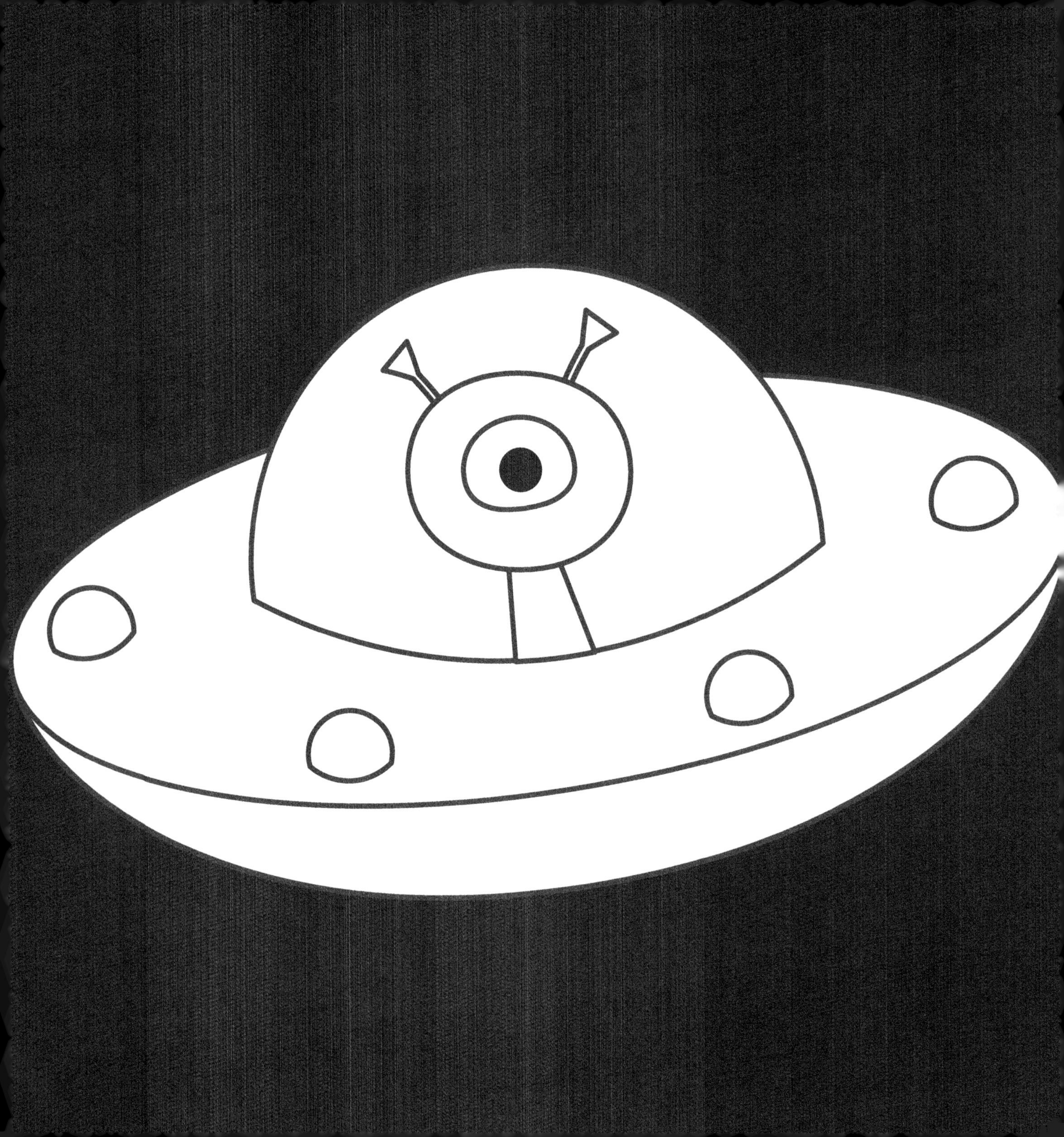

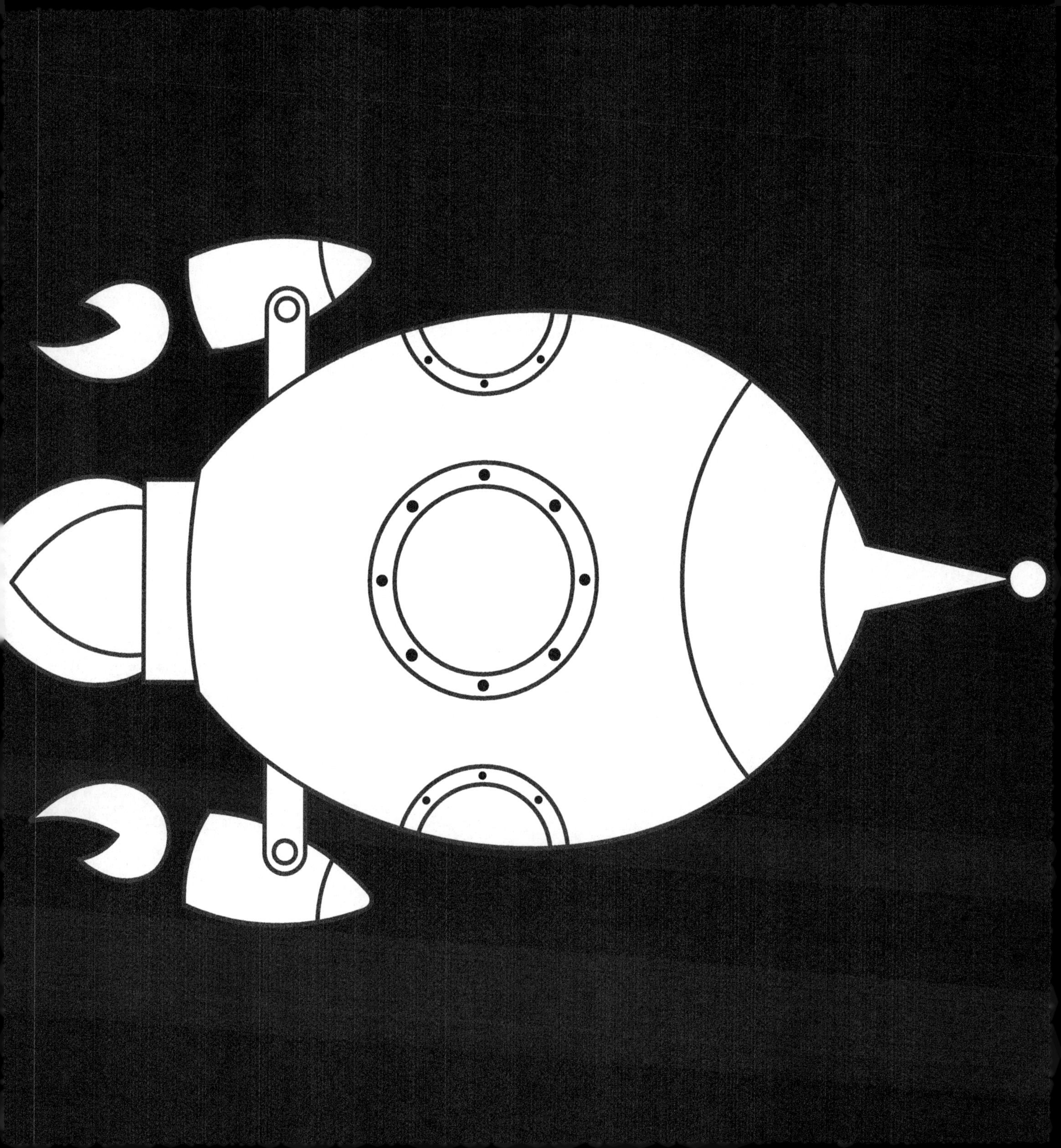

Printed in Great Britain
by Amazon

45103590R00020